Greek Mythology:

Legends of Greek Gods & Goddesses, Heroes, Ancient Battles & Mythical Creatures.

©Copyright 2018 by Cascade Publishing

All rights reserved.

It is not legal to reproduce, duplicate, or transmit any part of this document in either electronic means or in printed format. Recording of this publication is strictly prohibited.

CONTENTS

Introduction 1

Chapter 1. Why the Greeks? 5

Chapter 2. The Epochs of Greek Mythology 8

Chapter 3. Archaeological Sources of Greek Mythology 15

Chapter 4. A Gallery of Gods and Goddesses 22

Chapter 5. Early Greek Mythology – In the Beginning 31

Chapter 6. Gods and Humans 35

Chapter 7. All the Creatures Great and Small 39

Chapter 8. The Many Great Battles of Greek Myth 42

Chapter 9. Influences of Greek Mythology in Today's Culture 59

Conclusion 68

Introduction

Greek mythology ranks among the most important intellectual and cultural feats achieved by human civilization. The names Zeus, Troy, Medusa, and many others have permeated and affected both literature and human history for thousands of years. To highlight its importance, Greek mythology continues to be taught in practically every high school and major university in the United States. Harvard University, for example, has at least 10 courses in their Department of Classics that incorporate Greek mythology as its major lesson content. Given that among the authors of Greek mythology include intellectual giants like Plato, Sophocles, and Aristophanes, it should be no surprise that institutions such as Harvard see it as something worth learning about.

Why does Greek mythology have this much sway in human learning and storytelling? Why not the tales of other sects and cultures? How has it managed to stay relevant even after so much time has passed? Even today, we see its influence over in many different forms. Movies, plays, and television shows are still made about many of its stories and personalities, and a lot of its lessons and ideas are invoked and mentioned in diverse fields such as philosophy, politics, entertainment, literature, history, and even commerce.

There are many reasons.

First of all, the characters and events portrayed in Greek mythology tells us plenty about the time it was written. It gives us information about what our ancestors considered important, how they thought, and what their morals were. Greek mythology reflected the lifestyle and mentality of days long gone, by civilizations that were beginning to touch on the importance and consequence of human choices, relationships, beliefs, and most especially, imagination. It gives us valuable insight into what the human condition was at the time, in the same way that our activities we record today will provide historians of the future some understanding of how we lived.

Greek mythology encompasses such a wide range of characters and events that touches on every aspect of human existence. You name it, and Greek mythology talks of it: *Birth, life, death, morality, immortality, conflict, tragedy, loyalty, treachery, and respect.* Despite it having been written in ancient times, the lessons and drama that Greek mythology portrays reflect what it means to be human and in many cases, superhuman. Name any human trait and you can find a Greek mythology character or narrative that can be identified with it.

As part of this, the characters including the myth's powerful gods get wrapped in very human predicaments and circumstances—and then some. The stories are riveting, sometimes gory, what with castrations, the swallowing and spitting out of babies, chopping off heads, and casting off of all sorts of characters into the deep recesses of the netherworld. Many villains and monsters are downright terrifying, while many gods and mortals appeal to our all-too-human selves. They only seem perfect on the surface and their flaws eventually appear the more you read.

In conceiving the deities of their mythology, the Greeks

associated their gods with various aspects, desires, fears, and frailties of human life. For example, Hades was assigned to be the god of the dead, Ares the god of war, and Aphrodite the goddess of sexual desire. Some deities like Helios (the sun), Hestia (hearth), Apollo, and Dionysius were conferred a mixture of functions, purpose, and complex personalities. Together with location-specific characters such as the nymphs of caves and springs, and river gods, there is something for everyone to identify with to relate to their daily existence.

The characters from Greek mythology were truly the first superheroes—sometimes referred to as the blueprint of modern day versions such as Superman, Spiderman, The Hulk, and other superheroes that permeate today's pop culture scene. The villains of Greek mythology could also easily be the arch enemies of our modern-day comic book heroes. From Zeus hurling lightning bolts from high above, to Prometheus molding human beings from clay, many Greek gods possess extra-human powers that continue to generate awe and wonder. In a sense, they were the gods before the gods of organized religion.

Greek mythology not only tells of godlike beings who possess superpowers, it also shines a light on the common one—people who have no great power and are often at the mercy of the gods. It highlights many aspects of humankind that is still relatable today. The good things, the bad things—the failures and the victories. We are shown how even a simple human can overcome a powerful god with sheer ingenuity, so much so that they are eventually deified and given a seat amongst the constellations. This is one of the things that make Greek

Mythology beautiful, yet tragic.

For example, in the famous story of Troy which is discussed in Chapter 8, powerful gods and heroes were subject to the pressures, temptations, and everyday stresses of decision-making. It tested their strength and how they would respond in the direst of situations. People would be able to easily identify with mortals such as Odysseus, Jason, and Daedalus. Yes, the times differ, and the myths are a little exaggerated, but the themes remain the same.

Studying Greek mythology is a must for anyone who is interested in peering into the human soul, understanding history, and appreciating the creativity and imagination of humans long gone from our lives. I hope that my book can bring you to the window of wonder and fascination, and make you appreciate the wonders and excitement that our Greek ancestors have gifted us with.

Chapter 1.

Why the Greeks?

The Greeks were not the first civilization to come up with a spoken and written record about the stories of gods, heroes, and villains. The ancient Egyptians were actually the first humans to have left a record of their gods which were revered and feared by their civilization. The names of the Egyptian gods were uttered with equal amounts of reverence and dread. Egyptian deities like Isis, Osiris, and Hathor were omnipresent influences in the daily lives of ancient Egyptians. This is widely accepted as the very first piece of epic literature. Written works such as the Epic of Gilgamesh, which is of Babylonian and Sumerian origin, pre-dated the first Greek written manuscript by at least a thousand years.

So it truly is a feat for Greek mythology to have surpassed even these much older mythos. Even the word "mythology" is representative of the prevalence of Greek thought in a lot of modern thinking. The word comes from the Greek word 'mythos', which means "story of the people," and 'logos', which means speech or word. There are a few good reasons why Greek mythology has persisted as the most popular body of myth and epics in human civilization:

Greeks were the first real "thinkers" of human civilization. "Thinker" in this sense means that they not only brought forth novel ideas about mathematics, science, politics, and history, they were also the first group of humans to philosophize about human nature and thinking. They pioneered the art and science of intellectual conversation, education, knowledge, and how humans interact with the world and what's within it. This body of knowledge and thought permeated how they conceived their gods and their tales. Much of their intellectual and mythological output has directly shaped and impacted Western thought as we know it today.

The ancient Greeks were the first known international traders since their land was a gateway to the Mediterranean, and after expansion of their territory, trade with other countries became a key aspect of ancient Greek life. Further progress and migration of their people helped commerce to become more widespread, and all manner of manufactured goods, raw materials and food became available. This exposure to other cultures and materials also expanded the source material for their myths and legends especially those involving the sea and voyages across it. Their tales also became available to share with other people leading to their distribution to a much wider audience.

The "gods" that the ancient Greeks invoked in their tales were not used to impose morality and strict rules on their society. While the gods of Egypt and Christianity were "used" to control and shape society, the gods and immortals of the ancient Greeks, while perceived as influential on the lives of people, were not used as excuses to condemn or punish them. In comparison, violating the imagined dictates of the gods of ancient Egypt could lead to death, and the god of Moses and modern Christianity for a long time gave license for church leaders to excommunicate and even terminate the lives of people just for not believing church tenets.

The deities of the ancient Greeks on the other hand, were not deployed as hammers or levers to control daily living. For example, instead of dictating that its citizens exercise sobriety and temperance, the Greeks gave rise to Dionysius, the god of, winemaking, fertility and so-called "ritual madness" or drunkenness. So while Islam expressly prohibits alcohol, the ancient Greeks invented a god to promote it. As their deities were more friendly and down to earth, Greek mythology was more palatable and attractive to a wider audience.

Lastly, much of Greek mythology, while invoking gods with superhuman powers also touched upon the folly and glory of day to day human life. The ancient Greeks were the most advanced thinkers of their time and the lessons that their mythology taught were not only a window of their morality and thinking, they were also very instrumental in making modern humans contemplate on their condition as well. Aesop's fables for example, while not comprised of the fire and brimstone qualities of the epic confrontations of Greek mythology, offers practical lessons and thoughts on day to day living that are useful to this day.

Much can be learned from productive intellectual discourse and philosophy. No culture was better equipped towards this than the ancient Greeks who were the original purveyors of organized thought and teaching.

Chapter 2.

The Epochs of Greek Mythology

A casual observer of Greek mythology might assume that the master of the universe is Zeus, the omnipotent and omnipresent god of all gods. While his presence and influence were certainly important, he is but one among many hundreds of characters in the Greek mythology universe. To gain a proper understanding of Greek mythology, it is useful to divide it into sections that roughly coincide with the chronology of the origins of its characters. In this way, we can break down Greek mythology into three epochs which approximate its internal chronology.

The Age of Gods

This period starts with the beginning of life and approximates the Genesis story in the Christian Bible. It begins with the Chaos and the immediately resulting aftermath. In this period, the gods fought for their place in the heavens and on earth, and to assert their supremacy over nature and creation. This was the time before mortals (human beings) came into existence and when the gods lived amongst themselves, struggling and fighting over who gets to rule.

This epoch includes the creation myth, discussed fully in

Chapter 5 and the first generations of the spawn of Chaos who fought for supremacy in the world of deities. The term "gods" is a tricky application in Greek mythology. In a vast majority of religions and beliefs, a "god" usually meant an overpowering, omnipresent, and highly influential divine being, usually an inanimate spirit that was not made available to the five senses.

In Greek mythology however, these gods were not equal in power. Some of them were revered only in a few places and for very specific reasons. Then you have the deified mortals who do not possess any real power when compared to the Olympians or even the titans. Instead, what they had was something they were greatly admired and adored for. For example, Adonis could be considered the Kim Kardashian of ancient Greek mythology – he was famous just for being famous, and had no special powers at all except that he was a beautiful human specimen. The god Trophonius was mostly known for building the Oracle at Delphi with his brother, and actually died just after six days of finishing it. He is celebrated in annual festivals in a small town in Greece.

This system of gods is comparable to the system of saints in the Roman Catholic Church which has canonized hundreds of saints that are recognized as sacrosanct by the Church, but are well-known only in specific locations or represent some purpose. And like the Catholic saints, there are "major deities" who hold exalted places in the pantheon of Greek mythology.

The most famous of these "super-gods" are the Twelve Olympians who held sway over all creation. These twelve deities were central to the overall Greek worship of myths, while other cities and towns had gods that were only known in their specific locales. These small localized cults centered their legends, worship, and related activities on minor gods, nymphs, and other mythical creatures.

The Age of Gods and Men

When the gods created humans, the general tone of the relationship was one of distrust and fear. There was a great gap between them, and the mortals were usually portrayed as being subject to the mercy of the gods. This theme is quite comparable to the Judeo-Christian world after the fall of Adam and Eve: Humans generally lived in misery and toil, children routinely dishonored their parents, and each man sought only to serve their self-interests. The god/man era would be marked with themes related to "might meaning right" as the gods ruled with an iron fist over humankind. Despite such tumultuous times, however, you'll soon learn that there were mortals who challenged the gods that ruled over them. Some of them were even aided by the gods in battle, a feat that only few have achieved in these stories.

After the great battle of the gods, also known as the Titanomachy (discussed in more detail in Chapter 8), only the Olympians continued to populate the universe. It is during this time when Zeus gave tasked two Titans, Prometheus and Epimetheus, to create the first humans. Prometheus molded human beings out of clay, while another god, Athena the goddess of wisdom and craft, breathed life into his clay figures. Prometheus gave his brother, Epimetheus the task of providing all the earth's different beings varying skills and qualities such as: cunning, swiftness, agility, strength, fur, and wings.

Unfortunately, when it was time to give gifts to humans, the brothers discovered that Epimetheus had already given away many of the good qualities to non-human beings, leaving few—almost nothing—to mankind. Prometheus who loved humans more than the gods who banished his family to Tartarus, then took it upon himself to at least give humans the ability to stand up upright just as the gods could. He also decided to provide them with the gift of fire.

The Golden Age of Humans

This is the period where humans were said to have lived among the gods and also freely interacted with them. There was peace and harmony during this period, and humans lived a very long life without losing their youthful appearance. After they all died peacefully, their spirits went on to live in the afterlife serving as guardians to surviving humans.

Prometheus was very sympathetic to the human race, and seemed to care for mortals more than he did for the gods on Olympus. After all, the Olympians banished his family to Tartarus which left him bitter and lonely. When Zeus ordered all the gods to sacrifice some of their food to the deities, Prometheus thought of a scheme to fool Zeus. He created two separate servings of food. He created a serving of bones encased in juicy fat, and in the other, he filled some animal skin with the finest meats. When Prometheus asked Zeus to choose which serving he would consume, Zeus as expected, chose the serving with the bones thinking that it was accompanied with the finest meat. In his anger for being tricked by Prometheus, he took back fire from humans. He also decided that he had to punish Prometheus as well. This led to the Silver Age.

The Silver Age of Humans

Instead of living very long lives, men in the Silver Age only lived to around one hundred years, and their lives were also marked with animosity and strife with each other. They also lived under the control of their mothers. Men who refused to worship the gods were destroyed by Zeus. Still after death, humans were converted to blessed spirits and lived in the underworld.

Zeus' disdain for humans did not seem to have any limits in this Age. He directed one of the Olympians, Hephaestus, to create a beautiful human, Pandora, who was the first woman. Zeus then ordered Hermes, the messenger god, to "gift" Pandora with a lying tongue and a deceptive heart. To cap off his disdain for humans, Zeus provided Pandora with a box that unbeknownst to her admirer Epimetheus, contained disease, suffering, cruelty, and evil. Knowing of man's weakness of innate curiosity, Pandora opened the box and cursed the world by releasing all the evil things contained in it.

Zeus had left the human race defenseless and filled with weaknesses. They had no natural weapons with which to defend themselves. Still, Prometheus continued to be the protector of humanity and would stop at nothing to protect mortals. He resorted to deceit and stole reason from Athena, and gave back fire to humankind.

This affinity that Prometheus had for humans was not left unpunished by Zeus who decided to exact a heavy dose of punishment on the Titan. Zeus had him bound to a tree in the mountains of Caucasus and every night an eagle would come to tear out his liver. Once thought to have been condemned to an eternity of searing pain, Prometheus was eventually set free by Heracles (or Hercules).

The Bronze Age of Men

Zeus created the humans in the Bronze Age out of the ash tree. These humans were tough and hardened, and their main purpose in life was war. Their homes, tools, and armor were forged from bronze. Zeus' contempt for mortals were evident in the lives of men in this Age. They were undone because of their violent ways, and after death they were relegated to wandering spirits and left to suffer and rot in Hades, the Greek mythology equivalent of the Judeo-Christian hell.

This Age ended with the Greek mythology equivalent of Noah's flood, the flood of Deucalion.

The Heroic Age of Man

The age of heroes, this is where we find humankind finally bettering themselves, and becoming less fearful of the gods who have kept them bound for so long. This is also the time of many great battles, such as the ones fought in Troy and Thebes. When this race of humans died, they went to Elysium. Also called the Island of the Blessed, Elysium was a refuge for souls, it is where they would live a happy and blessed life for all eternity. Some traditions maintain that Zeus revived his father Cronus from the depths of Tartarus to rule over these souls.

The Iron Age of Man

This age is like the Silver and Bronze ages where humans live in misery and toil. In this Age, Zeus and all the other gods and goddesses will forsake mankind and Zeus himself will return one day to destroy this race. This is the race that the author of the Ages of Man, Hesiod, the author of the Greek creation tale, Theogony, included himself and all other humans in. It is a harsh version of the second coming of Jesus Christ, where Zeus himself will return one day to destroy all men as he has done in the past.

The Age of Human Heroes

While the impact and influence of the divine gods were significant, the mortal heroes of flesh and blood have also garnered significant interest among contemporary students of Greek mythology. The stories of the mortals in the Iliad and the Odyssey are much more identifiable to earth-bound mortals and contain many lessons for even modern day people. They're often far more preferred today than the Homeric Hymns and the deity-focused Theogony.

These mortal heroes would be on full display during the Trojan War and the Argonautica expedition; comprised of the mortal icons Jason the Argonaut, Helen of Troy, and of course, the god Heracles. Better known through his Roman name Hercules, this demigod provided help to Jason the Argonaut and other mortals whom he believed to be in the right side of the different conflicts.

There is much to enjoy about the tales of immortal gods and monsters. Just as much, there are also plenty of lessons to be learned.

Chapter 3.

Archaeological Sources of Greek Mythology

The material from which Greek mythology came from is varied and dispersed with many authors and traditions as its source. Like the Judeo-Christian bible, the compilation came from the efforts of many people cobbling together their works and thoughts over hundreds of years. The popularity of Greek mythology also becomes its worst enemy, because material for stories of a character can come from different sources with a vastly different portrayal of events.

Much of Greek mythology can be found in the writings of the great Greek thinkers. For example, in his work Cratylus, Plato talks about the golden race of men who came about during the kingship of Cronus. In this work, Plato clarifies that the Golden Age did not mean that humans were made from gold; instead, they were considered to be just as valuable because they were noble and good. Humans then were beneficent and cared about others, even after their death-- when they became guardians of the living.

Greek Mythology is basically a collection of stories told and passed down from the Ancient Greeks some through written works, whilst some were passed verbally. In other cases and in some places, what remains are traditions which are connected to these ancient myths. These stories also provided an outline of the different ritual and cultic practices at that time, but the highlights are the stories of the gods and heroes. These stories comprise a fairly large number of Greek mythology narratives that were originally communicated orally, but eventually became part of the ancient Greeks' written records.

The written record of Greek mythology comes primarily from the Classical period in Greece, circa 500 BC. While many of the stories behind the myths came from a much earlier time, written narratives of the myths did not exist before this Classical period. To summarize the archaeological record of Greek mythology therefore, most of Greek mythology as we know today was several hundred years' worth of hand-me-down narratives from a multitude of sources that finally found their way to written records in the Classical period. Our modern understanding of Greek mythology comes from the textual remains of this period.

But over the past hundreds of years, artifacts from archaeological dig sites and various other discoveries of pottery and other items, have added to the body of Greek mythology which validated most of what was in the written record.

Literary Sources

The earliest literary sources of Greek mythology are the two epic poems of Homer, the Odyssey and the Iliad which focuses on the events during and after the Trojan War. These two stories give us a strong indication of the ancient Greek propensity for fanciful, whimsical, and fantastic storytelling. But more compelling is the often antagonistic and complex relationship between the gods, and especially between the gods and humans. The written works first uncovered the Classical period and authored by Homer who was a prolific poet whose date of birth and existence is subject to much debate and discussion. There is a growing consensus that he lived around 800 BC.

His works were verbally transmitted and later converted into written formats between 800 and 600 BC, and some believe that Homer did the actual dictation. These written works were then split up into 24 so-called "rhapsodes" or books, and labeled by Greek alphabet letters. It is generally agreed upon that Homer's works were organized in Athens around 500 BC by the tyrant Peisistratos.

Around 150 BC the written versions of Homer's works were solidly established. The founding of the Library of Alexandria soon after allowed scholars such as Aristarchus, Zenodotus, and Aristophanes to come up with final, canonical versions of the texts.

The first printed version of Homer's work was produced in Milan in 1488. While this text helped the distribution of Homer's work to a much wider audience, modern scholars up to today search for other sources of his work, such as papyri and medieval manuscripts. This "multi-text view" has been the norm rather than the searching for a solitary definitive text. This approach for validating Greek mythology narratives have not been limited just to Homer's works but to those of others.

The other important source of ancient texts for Greek mythology was the Greek poet, Hesiod. Hesiod was a near-contemporary of Homer who was known to be a prolific writer and poet. His biggest contributions to Greek mythology were "Works and Days" and "Theogony" (Origin of the Gods) which contains the account of the creation of the world, the origin of, and the succession of the pantheon of Greek deities, the chronology of human ages, the origin of human suffering and turmoil, folktales, and on a more realistic level, the origin of sacrificial rituals. He also gives elaborate genealogies of each generation of the gods, including the giants and the Titans.

In "Works and Days," a poem about farming life, Hesiod includes narratives about gods that figured prominently in the genesis of humankind especially Pandora and Prometheus. In Chapter 2, we discussed part of the Four Ages of Men that chronicles the chronology of human existence from the time that Prometheus created the first human.

Aside from Homer and Hesiod, the archaeological written records include various literary treatments of the Greek gods by lyric poets such as *Bion, Theocritus, Simonides, Bacchylides, and Pindar of Thebes*, all of whom flourished between 600 and 500 BC.

It helped that both comic and tragic playwrights used the gods and human heroes of Greek mythology in their plots. Notable playwrights such as *Euripides, Sophocles, Aeschylus, and Aristophanes* were also part of this writing tradition and helped to add color to many characters and stories.

After the Classical Greek Age, writers from the Hellenistic Age (between 300 BC and 50 AD) and the Roman Age around this period corroborated many of the Greek mythology characters and tales through their writings. These included the works of Hellenistic poets *Parthenos, Callimachus, Rhodes, and Apollonius* as well as the great Roman writers *Ovid and Virgil*. Virgil wrote the "Aeneid," a story which is widely considered to be the third epic that the Trojan War inspired.

It was also during this period that so-called post-Homeric epics helped fill the gaps in the narratives of the Trojan War as recorded in the Iliad and the Odyssey. These consisted of shorter poems and rather than contradict Homer's original version of the Trojan War, they validated much of the original material.

Historical Works

While most of Greek mythology is understandably rooted in the lyrical tradition of poetry and other forms of literature, historians such as Diodorus Siculus and Herodotus; geographers such as Strabo and Pausanias provided alternative versions of the events in Greek mythology. They obtained these from local myths and various stories that they picked up during the travels around the Greek world.

Archaeological sources

It was through the archaeological digs of the German Heinrich Schliemann and the Briton Sir Arthur Evans that answers were brought to the many questions regarding the Greek myth's gods and heroes. Schliemann, an amateur archaeologist, uncovered artifacts for the Mycenaean civilization in the 19th century, while Evans discovered the Minoan civilization a century later. The artifacts discovered during these explorations provided much of the archaeological proof needed to put together details about Greek mythology.

The Schliemann excavations were able to unearth a small citadel mount which was about 100 feet deep. Subsequent studies of the dig also revealed 5o more buildings in 9 different groups, providing evidence that the site was inhabited by some of the earliest civilizations by around 3,000 BC until about 1400 AD. Future excavations would also turn up a once inhabited area that is about ten times the size of the original citadel. This dig, presumed to be the original location of Troy, provided archaeologists with plenty to study and look through. From scattered skeletons and charred debris, there were many indications that point to the destruction of the city as being a result of war. In Homer's lifetime, he may have known of this place and the events that transpired within it could have also inspired many of his works.

Other archaeological discoveries unearthed representations of Greek mythology in various media such as pottery, paintings, and depictions on various structures and edifices. Especially useful were vases and other artifacts discovered during the Greek Geometric period around 900 BC onwards. These contained depictions of various gods and heroes from Greek mythology.

All these different artifacts from the archaeological explorations and digs are important because they provide additional information for narratives, and characters that are not present in literary sources. This includes some of the more obscure narratives from the Trojan Wars and from the saga of Heracles or Hercules. These also help researchers assess the approximate dates of when the original literary compositions were made.

Chapter 4.

A Gallery of Gods and Goddesses

The challenge when it comes to cataloguing the different characters that are present in Greek mythology is attributed to their sheer number; the minor deities alone could easily number in the hundreds. In some cases, there are also overlapping identities which can cause further confusion for those trying to properly put each one in their right category. But such is the case when it comes to dealing with antiquity and its many stories. The work that goes into it will make any Olympian proud.

For this, the archaeological discoveries, together with the large amount of written records from several sources, does lend to some disadvantages. There is a fair amount of syncretism where the deities and heroes are both amalgamated and assigned different powers and characteristics. For example, you have the wine-god Dionysus. The general consensus when it comes to his worship is that he is the god of revelry and frenzy. This can be seen in the Bacchic rituals which are done in his honor. On the other hand, he is also portrayed as a wise god—far removed from the manic persona he is often associated with. This duality can be seen in many gods and goddesses throughout Greek Mythology.

Then, we must also consider the great number of "minor" gods and goddesses that figure very little in the overall scheme of Greek deities. In our list, we have included those who have been given fairly significant roles in the stories; whether it be because they were part of a god's retinue or if they have a myth solely of their own.

The Age of the Gods

Chaos – In Greek mythology, this can be likened to the scientific "Big Bang". While there is no artistic representation of Chaos, it is the origin of where things first came to be. Etymologically, chaos is a neutral noun that means "gap "or "yawning," but in the creation myth, it is represented by a being who bore children. It also represented another aspect of life, that of a gloomy, underground, and faraway place where the first things and beings came from.

Erebus – One of the five offspring of Chaos. It is the personification of darkness and is said to be the nether region where dead people pass through immediately after death.

Nyx –Born from Chaos in the beginning of creation. She is the first Greek goddess of the night.

Aether – The son of Erebus and Nyx, he is the god of the "upper air," or the pure air that the gods breathe. Mortals do not breathe this air.

Hemera – She is the daughter of Erebus an Nyx, and is the goddess of the daytime.

Thalassa – The daughter of Aether and Hemera, and the first goddess of the sea.

Gaia – Personified as "mother earth". It is from Gaia where all matter, living and inanimate, sprung from. She bore many "children," which dominated the universe of gods in Greek mythology: *Aergia, Ceto, Cyclops, Eurybia, the Gigantes, Hecatonchires, Nereus, the Ourea, Phorcys, Pontus, Pythong, Pontus, Titans, Thaumas, Typhon,* and her most prominent progeny, *Uranus*.

Uranus – The son/husband of Gaia. His main contribution to the pantheon of Greek deities is being father to the Titans.

Amalthea – Zeus' foster mother. She is honored by Zeus after her death by placing her in the heavens as a group of stars known as the constellation Capra. Her skin or that of her goat (this varies in different versions), was also turned into a protective aegis taken by Zeus in honor of her when she died, and became an artifact of protection in some traditions.

The Titans

Also called "The Overreachers," the Titans were the twelve progenies of Uranus and Gaia, and consisted of:

- ***Coeus***, the father of Leto, the mother of the Olympian Gods Apollo and Artemis.
- ***Crius***, the father of Astraeus.
- ***Cronus***, the youngest of the Titans, he is known to be the most deceitful, craftiest and most daring.

- ***Hyperion***, the father of Helios. He is often depicted as driving a fiery chariot across the sky, carrying with it the light of day.
- ***Iapetus***, the father of Prometheus.
- ***Mnemosyne***, a female and the embodiment of memory. The term "mnemonics" is named after her.
- ***Oceanus***, a male, and the eldest of the Titans. Oceanus is the god of both the primordial river which flows around to the edge of the world from the Underworld in a never-ending, circular stream.
- ***Phoebe***, an early goddess of the moon.
- ***Rhea***, a female and an earth goddess who would later become mother of the Olympian Gods. Together with Cronus, they would sire many major gods.
- ***Tethys***, the most ancient goddess of the sea.
- ***Theia***, an early goddess of light.
- ***Themis***, a female and another earth or mother goddess.

The Olympians

If you're wondering, Mount Olympus is a real place in Greece. It is located between Macedonia and Thessaly. It is also Greece's highest peak, and was the first location designated as a national park by Greece in 1938.

But the Mount Olympus we often read of in Greek mythology is a lot more popular than its real-world counterpart. In Greek mythology, Mount Olympus served as home to the Olympians—hence the name. The Olympians are the gods and goddesses who reigned over the earth after the Titans have been defeated, and sent off to Tartarus. Led by Zeus, they presided over many different activities and virtues. They also represented many different aspects of human life. *They are as follows*:

- **Aphrodite** – The goddess of beauty, desire, procreation, and passion. One of Zeus' daughters, she married Hephaestus but had numerous adulterous affairs, the most notable of which was with Ares. The sex-related words venereal and aphrodisiac comes from her name.
- **Apollo** – A god that represents a multitude of things. He is known as the god of light, the sun, healing, medicine, the arts, inspiration, truth, philosophy and prophecy. He is the son of Zeus and Leto.
- **Ares** - Most notable for being the god of war. He was an important product of the union between and Hera. However, because of his predisposition towards violence and overall unruly attitude, he was despised by all the other gods.
- **Artemis** – The goddess of all animals, virginity, birth, the forests and the moon. She is also a protector to young maidens. Artemis is the daughter of Leto and Zeus and is Apollo's twin sister.
- **Athena** – The goddess of reason, knowledge, intellect, and wisdom. She is the daughter of the Oceanid, Metus, and Zeus.
- **Demeter** – The goddess of the seasons, nature, and the harvest, she presides over the earth's fertility and grains. She is the middle daughter of Rhea and Cronus. Demeter

also became one of Zeus' many lovers, and is the mother of Persephone.

- **Dionysus** – The god of wine, fertility, madness and celebrations. He is a son of Zeus and Semele, a mortal. He is the youngest god in Olympus and the only god to have been born of a mortal mother, Semele.
- **Hades** – The eldest son of Rhea and Cronus, he is god of the underworld, which was also eventually named after him. Together with his brothers Poseidon and Zeus, they defeated the Titans, their father's generation of gods, and won control over the universe.
- **Hephaestus** - The god of volcanoes, invention, and craftsmanship. He is the son of Zeus and Hera. He is also married to Aphrodite. The word volcano comes from his Latin name, Vulcan.
- **Hera**   - Queen of all the gods and the goddess of family, marriage, childbirth, and women. She is the youngest daughter of Rhea and Cronus and Rhea, and is the sister-wife of Zeus. As the marriage goddess, she often tried to exact revenge on his philandering husband Zeus' lovers as well as the children borne from his many affairs. She is often portrayed as a very vengeful character.
- **Hermes** – The god of games, thieves, travel, and commerce. He was the messenger of the gods. Hermes was the son of nymph, Maia who coupled with Zeus. After Dionysius, he is the second-youngest Olympian.
- **Persephone** – She is daughter of the harvest goddess Demeter and Zeus. As wife to Hades, she reigns as queen of the underworld. Though she and her husband do not

reside in Mount Olympus like the other gods, they are often counted among their number.

- ***Poseidon*** – The god of the seas, earthquakes, hurricanes, storms, and water. He is the middle son of Rhea and Cronus. Brother of Zeus and Hades. Like Zeus, he had many lovers although was married to Amphitrite, a Nereid.
- ***Zeus*** - The ruler of Mount Olympus and the king of all the gods. He was also known as the god of thunder, lightning, the sky, justice, and law and order. Zeus gained reputation as the greatest god on Olympus even if he was the youngest offspring of Rhea and Cronus. Despite being married to the goddess Hera, you'll learn that throughout mythology, Zeus took on many lovers—both mortal and immortal. A habit, which has caused plenty of trouble for the women he had coupled with.
- ***Leto*** - daughter of the Titans Phoebe and Coeus and Phoebe, she is the sister of Asteria and the mother, Apollo and Artemis by Zeus.

Gods, Humans, and Heroes

- ***Heracles*** – Also called Hercules in the Roman tradition. He is among the greatest of the heroes in Greek mythology. He is a son of Zeus, and championed the Olympian cause against the chthonic monsters.
- ***Theseus*** – The mythical founder of Athens and a hero to the ancient Greeks. He is said to have slayed the Minotaur, a large monster with the head of a bull and the body of a man. Theseus used the sword that his father Aegeus had given him to slay the monster. The Minotaur

was kept in a labyrinth were many young maidens were sacrificed by King Minos in order to appease the monster.

- **King Minos** – A son of Zeus and the first king of Crete. He became the judge of dead spirits in the Underworld after his death. The Minoan civilization was named after him by archaeologists.
- **Icarus** – The son of Daedalus, the master craftsman who created the Labyrinth which held the dreaded Minotaur. Icarus tried to flee Crete using wings that his father had made from feathers held together by wax. Daedalus forewarns Icarus and tells him not to fly too high (the sun would melt the wax) or too low (the dampness of the sea would clog the operation of the wings). But Icarus ignored his father and flew extremely high anyway. The heat from the sun melted the wax holding the wings together and Icarus fell into the sea. His story is often used as an example for hubris and its consequences.
- **Pandora** – Her name means "all gifts". She was the first woman created by the Gods. We know of her as the woman who released many ill things into the world after giving into her curiosity.
- **Achilles** – One of Greek Mythology's greatest warriors, and the central character in Homer's Iliad. His parents were the mortal Peleus and his mother was the goddess Thetis. Peleus was a king of the Myrmidons, a race of people supposedly created by Zeus from a colony of ants. Stories tell that Achilles, as a young baby, was dipped by his mother in the River Styx. As his mother held him by the foot while submerging the rest of his body, his heel

was not touched by the river and this became his sole weakness. He died after receiving an arrow to this specific part of the body—but not before winning plenty of battles and cementing himself as one of the heroes of the Trojan War.

- **Prometheus** – This god's name means "forethought". Prometheus is a Titan who created mankind and is its biggest benefactor. Among other things, he stole fire from Mount Olympus and gave it to human beings.
- **The Oracle at Delphi** – The high priestess of Apollo's temple at Delphi who served as an oracle, seer, and prophet. She was consulted by many characters in Greek mythology including Lycurgus and Oedipus.

Chapter 5.

Early Greek Mythology – In the Beginning

In Chapter 2, we had a glimpse of the various stages of Greek mythology and the major characters that populated each epoch. It is useful however, to examine how each of its many different gods and goddesses came into being. Also of interest is how human beings were woven into the overall scheme of events.

Every major religion has its own creation story, there are different versions of how the universe and all within it was created and this varies depending the beliefs one practices. Greek mythology has its own "creation stories," and you'll find that there are also many similarities between it and the others.

In Greek mythology it was Hesiod, considered one of the first poets in human history to have ever left records of what he named were poems, who first wrote about how all life may have began. In this sense he is the equivalent of Moses in the Judeo-Christian tradition. Major religions have to come up with how heaven, earth, and humans materialized and where the Judeo-Christian specify that the world was created in a certain way in six days, Greek mythology does not go into much detail about how and for how long creation took place.

Hesiod's poem, the *Theogony or Theogonía* in Greek, meaning "the birth or genealogy of the gods" was composed around 700 B.C. According to Hesiod, everything began with Chaos, a gaping nothingness and void. From this void came Gaia, whether she was born of Chaos or materialized on her own, it is not touched on. Gaia was a prolific god that begat many other gods. From Chaos also came Eros, the god of love, the dreaded Tartarus, or the terrifying and grim abyss below the earth, and Erebus. But it was from Gaia where many of Greek Mythology's deities were born. Among her children where the Titans and the Cyclops who are among the most popular characters in Greek folklore.

Gaia, personified as a big-bosomed woman, begat many progeny, but her most significant contribution was Uranus, who eventually also became her husband. It should be noted that Gaia's first children, including Uranus, were born through parthenogenesis Or the birthing of progeny from just a single gender.

With Uranus, Gaia gave birth to the first set of Titans comprised of six males: Oceanus, Iapetus, Hyperion, Cronus, Crius, and Coeus; and six females: Tethys, Themis, Theia, Rhea, Phoebe, and Mnemosyne. After this prolific coupling, Uranus and Gaia decreed that no more Titans were to be born. Still, Gaia bore more children and the titans were eventually followed by the birth of the Hecatonchires: *Briareus, Cottus, and Gyges.*

These three were monstrous looking giants with a hundred hands and fifty heads; they were so strong and terrible in nature that even their father Uranus found them revolting. In fact, he hid them away somewhere within the earth, to avoid chaos at their hands. He also did the same to his other three offspring known as the Cyclops, who were also giants, with a single eye on their foreheads. Uranus threw the Hecatonchires into Tartarus, which angered Gaia, who then ordered Cronus to castrate his own father. Gaia and Cronus set up a plan and eventually managed to ambush the hateful Uranus. Cronus sliced off his father's genitals with a sickle and cast it into the ocean. Because Uranus had been castrated, Cronus was crowned to be the ruler of the Titans, with Rhea becoming his sister-wife.

This event marks the beginning of the tumultuous relationships between the titans and the gods. Particularly with Cronus, who was ever fearful that his children would commit the same treachery against him. To avoid this, the Titan made sure to consume all his offspring with Rhea immediately after they were born; snatching them up and eating them as soon as they came out. Of course, as a mother, Rhea did not take too kindly to this and much like Gaia before her, the Titaness, devised a plan that would put an end to Cronus' reign of terror. To save their youngest son, she swaddled a rock in a baby's blanket when Zeus was born, and Cronus ended up swallowing the stone instead of Zeus.

Rhea would get some measure of revenge after Zeus reached maturity. The young god drugged a drink that Cronus took, and the concoction made Cronus vomit up all his children that he ate together with the stone. Cronus threw up his swallowed children in reverse order of when he ate them. In their gratitude, the Cyclops provided Zeus with lightning bolts as weapons—which eventually became the symbols most associated with him. In fact, many artistic renditions of Zeus often portray him as carrying a bolt or bolts of lightning in his hands.

After saving the swallowed children, Cronus was challenged by his own son for the right to rule over the gods. Together with his siblings, they defeated Cronus and the other Titans in a battle that was to be known as the "Titanomachy". After the dust has settled, the Titans were locked away in Tartarus for their punishment.

This battle is further recounted in Chapter 8.

Chapter 6.

Gods and Humans

Not all the major characters in Greek mythology had special super-human powers. Not all of them were immortal, held court in the heavens or somewhere in the supernatural ether. The most compelling narratives in Greek mythology talk about the divine intervention by immortal deities in mortal affairs. In this chapter, we will look at the more notable stories involving mortals in their struggles and associations with the deities that control their lives.

We have learned that after the gods got tired of being amongst other deities, they created humans and began a period when gods and men began to mingle freely with each other. The most common types of involvement consisted of gods seducing and even raping mortal women which sometimes resulted in demigod offspring; however, it must be noted that not all of these half-god, half-men beings were of heroic nature. In some cases, such as when it came to Ares' progeny, they were also the cause of strife for others, and were the villains in many stories.

Zeus and His Many Mortal Lovers:

Aside from being the King of the Gods, Zeus is also quite well-known for another thing—his many affair. Despite being the only god who is officially married, he continued consorting with other deities and mortals as well.

His coupling with Danae, the only offspring of King Acrisius and his wife, Queen Eurydice of Argos, produced the hero Perseus, who is famous for slaying the despised Medusa among many other quests he has been on. Zeus also had a child with Alcmene, who was already married at the time of their coupling. She bore Zeus a son, Heracles. A name most Greek Mythology enthusiasts would be quite familiar with as there are plenty of stories about his adventures and victories. Zeus also had an infamous tryst with Callisto, a mortal princess from the south of Greece. Her claim to fame, aside from being another of Zeus' victims, was that she was transformed into a bear by an angry Hera (Zeus' wife), in which form she gave birth to a son, Arcas.

Callisto's story has quite the bittersweet ending. Arcas, in time, grew up to become a great hunter. It was this ill-fated adventure that would bring mother and son together again, but it would be their last time as well. Seeing her son after so long, Callisto rushed to greet him. Thinking that the bear was running towards him to attack, Arcas shot an arrow into Callisto and killed her. Upon finding out what he had done, Arcas pleaded with the gods. Zeus took pity on the two and raised them to the heavens, becoming what we now know as the constellations as Ursa Major and Ursa Minor, or the big and small bears.

One would think that these affairs, many of which happened out of deceit on Zeus' part, would have been despised by the mortals. Some did, but not everyone was of the same mind. His other mortal conquests included dozens of other humans some of which were relatives of kings and queens who welcomed the prospect of their daughters bearing the progeny of the king of all kings, Zeus. A connection to the gods, after all, was power.

It must also be said that it isn't just the male gods who coupled with mortal men, and women. Even the goddesses had their fair share of lovers, with Aphrodite in particular having the most number. Much like Zeus, she seduced and deceived mortals in order to get what she wanted. Such is the case that produced her mortal son, Aeneas, who eventually became one of Greek Mythology's most famous warriors. Of course, we cannot forget the story of Achilles who is the son of the goddess Thetis and the mortal Peleus. He is, after all, the most renowned of all the heroes in these stories—remaining undefeated and victorious until his tragic death.

Gift from the Gods - Invention and Knowledge:

The relationship between gods and humankind isn't always so terrible; in most cases, it is also beneficial for both sides. This is very true in times of war when gods would take sides and actually assist their chosen group towards victory. During times of peace, however, they also provided mankind with useful tools and know-how, allowing them to improve themselves and the way they live life. Some of the most noteworthy instances of such includes:

- Prometheus stealing fire from the gods because he felt that humans were shortchanged when talents and powers were being handed out;
- Athena and Apollo teaching mankind arts and crafts;

- Dionysus providing people with the knowledge of wine-making and;
- Demeter teaching agriculture and how to better make use of the land for food.

The Amazons

We've heard of the Athenians, and of the Trojans. We know that there were races of men who had the reputation of being fierce warriors – always winning in the battlefield whether it be with the guidance of the gods or not. The Amazons were no different, except, unlike these other groups of people, they were an all-female culture. These powerful women were renowned for their superior battle skills, and could match and even surpass males in strength and ability.

The Amazons lived in an independent society which was fully separate from mankind. They could mate with males, but could never allow these men to integrate into their culture. Given that it is female-dominated, any males who lived with them would only function as servants, assigned to do only menial tasks. The Amazons spent most of their waking hours training extensively for battle, making them always ready for any attack.

Ares, the god of war, was their patron god, which was appropriate because of the Amazons' warrior culture. Ares was known to have fathered some of the Amazons' greatest queens. In the Trojan War, the Amazons followed Ares and joined the Trojans in battle. The Amazons also honored Artemis who symbolized the hunt, and is a figure of womanly strength in Greek Myth—much like Athena, herself.

Chapter 7.

All the Creatures Great and Small

So now that we've gotten better acquainted with the gods and the humans who were part of the Greek Mythology universe, let's move on to some of the other beings that comprise this often fantastic, sometimes terrifying world.

- ***Gorgons*** – In Greek and maybe even Sanskrit, the word means "dreadful. The Gorgons were comprised of three sisters, and the term is most associated with MEDUSA. They were let loose in the world to spread terror and fear. They take the form of a winged female human, with live venomous snakes on their head instead in of hair. Those unfortunate enough to look at their horrifying faces immediately turn into stone.
- ***Medusa*** – One of the scariest characters in Greek mythology, while she is usually portrayed as a woman, Medusa is considered a Gorgon monster. She was beheaded and killed by Perseus, the son of Zeus and the mortal Danae. However, she wasn't always this way – becoming a gorgon was a punishment from Athena. A rather undeserved one at that; Medusa was attacked in the goddesses temple by the ocean-god Poseidon as she was worshipping in Athena's temple. The goddess saw

this as an offense (she is a virgin-god), and instead of punishing her uncle for the act, turned her wrath on Medusa instead.

- **Nymphs** – These are minor female immortal divine spirits that live in specific landforms or locations. They are nature deities who represented different aspects of nature and also took on the appearance of where they lived. They usually resided in lakes, streams, forests, and mountainous regions. Nymphs are often depicted as young, nubile, and beautiful women who loved to sing and dance, and are the inspiration for the fairies of other folklore. Also among the nymphs were the Nereids who formed part of Poseidon's court.

- **Oceanids** – Nymphs who populated the seas. They are the 3,000 daughters of Tethys and Oceanus. Each Oceanid was a patroness of a cloud, flower, pasture, pond, lake, sea, river, or spring.

- **Meliae** – Tree nymphs that were created from the semen or blood that was scattered on earth when Uranus was castrated by Cronus.

- **Pegasus** – This winged horse sprang from Medusa's neck but eventually flew Perseus to safety after Medusa's two sisters chased him after he decapitated his sister.

- **Harpies** – Half-bird, half-men flying creatures, whose name means "snatchers". They take evildoers from the earth and bring them to the netherworld even as they steal their food.

- **Cyclops** – These are race of one-eyed giants that existed before humans were created. The term "cyclops" means "round eyes." They served in a variety of functions during the ages of the gods to serve them: Warriors, craftsmen, and builders.

- **Erinyes** – Minor female deities of the Underworld. Also called infernal goddesses whose primary role were to torment men based on the whims of the gods.
- **Gigantes** - Offspring of Gaia who were formed from the blood that spilled from Uranus when he was castrated by Cronus. They were a race of giant beings who were feared for their aggression, size, and great strength.

Chapter 8.

The Many Great Battles of Greek Myth

The most interesting and riveting aspects of Greek mythology is the narration of battles involving both deities and mortals. These battles usually pitted the forces of good versus evil, which makes it easy to root for one side and despise the other. The confrontations often conveyed some sense of morality or comeuppance for the protagonists. In many cases, one is left with a feeling that all sides in a war or battle can be losers because of the sacrifices that need to be made in the name of victory.

The Titanomachy

This battle was, chronologically, the first great battle in Greek mythology because it involved the first generations of gods that came out of Chaos in the creation story. This was a ten-year battle amongst the gods, and it happened even before the first mortal being was created. The battle was waged to determine who would rule the universe. It was a battle between the titans and the first generation of young gods, which and resulted in the banishment of the latter and the rise of the twelve Olympians. The Titanomachy is also more popularly known as the Battle of the Titans or Clash of the

Titans, versions of which have been depicted in major novels, movies, and other media.

How it Began:

As described in Chapter 5, the stage for this titanic clash was set after Cronus the youngest Titan, overthrew his father Uranus with the assistance of Gaia, his mother. Gaia was angered when Uranus imprisoned her children in Tartarus and convinced Cronus and his brothers to have Uranus castrated.

TO carry out this castration, Gaia fashioned a huge sickle and assembled Cronus with his brothers and ordered them to use the sickle to castrate Uranus. But only Cronus agreed to do the castration. Gaia gave Cronus the sickle, and set up Uranus for an ambush. When Uranus next saw Gaia, Cronus assaulted Uranus and cut off his genitals with the sickle that Gaia forged, and cast his genitals into the sea. The blood from Uranus' castration spilled on the earth and gave rise to Meliae, Erinyes, and Gigantes or Giants. From the blood or semen of his severed genitals, Aphrodite rose from the sea.

By castrating Uranus, Cronus became the King of the Titans, and ascended to the throne. He solidified his hold on power when he dispatched his siblings, the Cyclops and the Hecatonchires to Tartarus. This action however had its consequences. Uranus had prophesied that one among Cronus' offspring would stage a revolt against him in the same way that he had rebelled against his father. Cronus was ever fearful of his reign and became a much more terrible king than his father, Uranus. To prevent the prophecy from coming true, he swallowed all of his children except for the youngest—

Zeus-- after Rhea managed to conceal him by tricking Cronus to swallow a rock wrapped in a blanket instead.

Rhea then brought Zeus to Crete and he is raised by Amalthea, widely known to be Zeus' foster mother. When he became an adult, he returned to the seat of his mother and father, winning a place for himself as Cronus' cupbearer. When he gains the trust of Cronus, he tells Metis to make Cronus drink a mixture of wine and mustard that will cause Cronus to vomit and throw up all the children that he swallowed. After he frees his siblings, he leads them in revolt against Cronus and the Titans. Zeus' "team" includes Poseidon, Hades, Hera, Demeter, and Hestia who were all previously swallowed by Cronus.

Zeus also releases the Cyclops and the Hecatonchires from their banishment in Tartarus, and the beasts join him in the revolt. The Cyclops forged lightning and thunder for him, while the Hecatonchires threw huge rocks at the approaching enemy. The remaining Titans helped Cronus in defending his crown—all, except for Prometheus and Themis. This battle ensued for ten years before Zeus' army eventually triumphed. After his victory, Zeus imprisoned the vanquished in Tartarus and the Hecatonchires became their guards. One of the Titans who fought with Cronus, Atlas, was meted out special punishment. He was ordered to hold up the sky for eternity.

After the victory the three brothers Zeus, Hades, and Poseidon divided the universe between themselves. Hades is awarded the Underworld, Poseidon the ocean and all the waters, and Zeus, all the air and the sky. The other gods on the victorious side were given specific powers according to their nature. Those gods left on earth were allowed to carry on as they pleased, except when Hades, Poseidon, or Zeus were called on to intervene.

Some narratives indicate that Zeus gave the Titans their freedom after he secures and consolidates his power.

The Trojan War

The Trojan War is, without a doubt, the definitive and most iconic war account in Greek mythology; not only because it is one of the biggest, but also because it put the spotlight on Greek Myth's most popular heroes. The Trojan War's major players include gods, demigods, monsters, human heroes, and villains embroiled in a long-running saga of conspiracy, deceit, murder, widespread destruction, appalling and heartbreaking deaths, and of course, inspiring redemption and victory. The totality of the tale of Trojan Wars did not come from just one writer or account (even if Homer is the most significant source for the narration because of The Iliad), but from various corroborative textual and archaeological sources. One single authoritative work does not cover all the details of the full story of the Trojan War.

There is no other story in human civilization except for the stories in the Old Testament and the story of Jesus Christ in the Judeo-Christian tradition that has inspired artists of every kind and predisposition. Greek educators make reading and understanding the narratives of the Trojan War compulsory classroom and study material.

How it Began:

The story begins in about 1200 BC when a jilted Menelaus, King of Sparta and brother of Agamemnon the King of Mycenae, assembled an expedition to retrieve his wife, Queen Helen who had run off with Paris, a prince of Troy along with a massive amount of Spartan treasure. Agamemnon was, at the time, the most powerful leader in Greece while Helen was the daughter of Leda (from her union with Zeus) and Tyndareus, and considered to be the most beautiful woman of her day. Her father together with all the Greek warriors, promised to avenge any insult to her.

Agamemnon called for the help of a number of Greek heroes, including: Ajax, Nestor, Odysseus (in Roman myth, Ulysses), and the famed warriors Achilles and Diomedes, the king of Anatolia. With a fleet of over a thousand Spartan ships, they crossed the Aegean Sea and landed in Troy, demanding the return of Helen by the Trojan king, Priam. Priam was the son of Laomedon who was given the city of Troy by the gods Apollo and Poseidon.

Priam refuses their demands and the Spartans invoked the oath that Tyndareus had made with regards to Helen. The Greeks put together a massive army to invade Troy, but to do this, they must first assemble and leave from Aulis, near the southern part of Greece. The contingent at Aulis was led by great Greek warrior Achilles, who was also part of the prophecy that Troy, one that says the city will only be conquered under his command. However, due to some disagreements with the Greeks, Achilles is forced to leave the battle temporarily.

The invading contingent was then put under Agamemnon's leadership who, through a rather impious boast, managed to draw the ire of Artemis. As punishment, the goddess sent strong contrary winds to hinder the invading fleet, and Agamemnon had to offer his daughter Iphigenia in sacrifice to appease Artemis who then allowed the Greek fleet to sail on.

The first Greek warrior who landed on the shore, Protesilaus, was killed by the great Trojan warrior and general Hector. After they landed the Greeks attempt another shot at diplomacy and send a contingent to retrieve Helen and the treasure. When the Trojans refused again, the Greeks moved to entrenched themselves for a siege that would last almost ten years. It is during the 10th year of the battle where many of the tales highlights begin to unfold:

- Agamemnon insults Apollo by kidnapping Chryseis, a daughter of one of Apollo's prophets. An enraged Apollo sends down a nine-day plague on the Greek army. Achilles, with intervention of Zeus, convinces Agamemnon to return the girl and stop the plague.
- A duel between Paris and Menelaus results in Aphrodite saving Paris just as he is about to be killed. The protagonists survive the duel.
- Achilles kills a number of Trojans soldiers single-handedly, and in some narratives, became the lover of Helen, Medea, and Polyxena, daughter of Priam.
- Odysseus and Diomedes kill 13 Trojan allies and steal many horses.
- Hector records several successes against the Greeks including: breaching their ramparts and setting their ships on fire. He later manages to kill Patroclus who is a

close friend of Achilles; he achieves this through the help of Apollo. However, Hector is also later killed by Achilles in yet another battle, after the latter returns to battle in order to avenge is beloved friend's death.

- Achilles is given a suit of "divine armor" by Hephaestus upon the request of his mother Thetis.

- Also, in the tenth year of the battle, the Amazons join the Trojan forces. Their leader, Queen Penthesilea is killed by Achilles in battle. In the same skirmish, he also manages to slay the King of Ethiopia, Memmon who had also recently joined with the Trojans. Achilles is finally killed when Paris pierces his heel with an arrow, the only part of his body that is vulnerable to an attack.

- Paris does not survive this war, too. He is finally killed by Philoctetes from an arrow shot from the bow of Hercules.

- The Greeks use the "Trojan Horse," a massive hollow wooden structure that was filled with armed Greek warriors. The Greeks pretended to abandon the war and left the wooden horse in its place, spreading false rumors that it is a valuable trophy to them. The Trojans took the bait and brought the horse into the city. When the signal was given, the Greek army inside the horse began their ambush, destroying the city and murdering King Priam, together with Hector's infant son, Astyanax.

- Ares was the god of war and the goddess Athena, famed for her brilliance in war strategy, joined the battle in the name of justice. She favored non-violent means to settle disputes, but should there be no other recourse, the goddess does participate in battle. During the Trojan War, she sided with the Greeks and faced off with Ares who took the Trojan's side. Diomedes faced off with Ares and Athena aided Diomedes by using the helm of invisibility that he borrowed from Hades. The helm caused Ares' spear to veer off course when it was hurled towards Diomedes. This gave Diomedes the opportunity to launch a counter-attack against the god, who he was able to seriously wound. Ares was eventually forced to leave the battlefield, and returned to Mount Olympus where he was tended to by Zeus.

The Aftermath:

Because Troy was given to mortals as a gift from the gods, the gods considered the sacking of the city as a sacrilege destroyed most of the Greek fleet as they journeyed back from Troy. In the return voyage, Agamemnon was murdered by his wife and her lover. Cassandra, who was the king's mistress at the time, was also murdered by the same people.

Odysseus has many historic post-Trojan war adventures, dwarfing most of the other survivors. He sets out and loses many ships due to a series of unfortunate events because the Greeks had angered Poseidon. He kills a Cyclops monster and was able to speak with Achilles' spirit. Upon returning home, he found his palace surrounded by suitors waiting for his wife's hand in marriage—every loyal to him, she refused them all. Odysseus murdered each one of the men, along with the female servants in his home for laying with the unwanted guests.

After they are defeated by the Trojans, the remaining Greek heroes began to make their way home. It takes Odysseus ten years to make the storied and arduous journey back to his waiting family. This voyage back to Ithaca is narrated in Homer's "The Odyssey".

Helen, whose actions and affair with Paris started the epic war in the first place, returned back home to Sparta, and became queen to Menelaus once again. Some accounts tell of her banishment to the island of Rhodes after the death of Menelaus, and that she met her death by hanging upon the orders of a vengeful war widow.

The great Roman poet Virgil who like most followers the Trojan War were left enthralled by its scope and spectacle, authored "The Aeneid," which tells of a group of Trojans led by the Trojan hero Aeneas who flee their destroyed city and proceed to Carthage to establish the city of Rome, assigning some sort of origin story to approximate the impressive myths originated by the Greeks.

The Quest for the Golden Fleece:

While not a battle in the sense of a single epic showdown, the story of Jason and the Argonauts is still a gripping tale of bravery and heroism. It is among some of the most iconic tales of Ancient Greece.

In this much retold story, Jason from Argo arrives in his hometown of Iolcus to find out that the throne of his father, Aeson, has been usurped by his uncle Pelias. In order to restore throne to his father, Jason agrees to retrieve the Golden Fleece from Colchis, which is located across the treacherous Black Sea. The Golden Fleece is the hide and hair of a winged, golden ram and is the ultimate symbol of kingship and authority.

To cross the treacherous sea, Jason decides that he must fashion a suitable ship for the voyage. He enlists the help of the ship maker Argus, who then gets to work on a ship that is capable of providing prophecies as well as communicate. The ship is named Argo, and Jason's crew were called the Argonauts. However, one of the most interesting parts of the story is the crew itself—it is no ordinary set of men that rode with Jason during this voyage.

The crew was comprised of many sons of gods, including Heracles or Hercules, the son of Zeus and one of the mightiest deities in Greek mythology. This crew of men also included the Greek god, Pollus, who would play a significant role in the many battles that they would encounter during their Golden Fleece voyage.

On their way to Colchis, the Argonauts had to face many challenges in the various islands they passed through. These included Lemnos, Doilones, Cius, where they had to leave Hercules behind; Bebryces. Bosporus, which was ruled by Phineas, the Symplegades which are really two massive stone structures which crush ships that try to pass through them, only to later encounter feisty Amazons, which they pretty much avoid—but barely.

But not every battle was avoidable. During their voyage, they also ended up battling Harpies, gigantic creatures, and other obstacles strewn along their way. When they finally arrived in Colchis, King Aeëtes tells that Jason he can have the Fleece just as long he completes three nearly impossible tasks. These included killing a terrifying dragon guarding the Golden Fleece, and defeating ones that sprout out from the earth. With the help of Hera, and Aeëtes' daughter Medea, Jason is able to complete the tasks and sail back to Iolcus in triumph.

The Revolt of the Giants:

After Zeus and his brothers assumed control of Greece, they had to deal with the revolt of the giants. There were twenty-four giants who participated in the attack, and because of their size and great strength, the Olympians grew fearful. The Giants staged their assault by stacking up several mountains, using these as makeshift stairs in order to help them reach the peak of Mount Olympus where the ruling gods resided.

Hercules, who was earlier prophesied to be the one to prevent this revolt against the Olympians, appeared in the midst of the battle. He struck down one of the giant with an arrow, but it didn't do much damage. The giant was able to withstand the attack and stand up again. Athena soon figured out that the Giant survived because they were in their "native" ground—the mountains made of stone. Athena, after realizing this, ordered Hercules to take the Giant to a different place where they could not be revived once struck down. This gave the gods leverage and after many battles, the superior strength of the Olympians to came out victorious over the Giants.

Perseus and Medusa:

The Oracle at Delphi tells the king of Argos, Acrisius that his own grandson would murder him one day and that his would-be killer will be a child of Danae, his daughter. To protect himself from this prophecy, he imprisons Danae in an underground chamber so that she could not mate and have children.

However, Zeus appears as a shower of golden rain and breaches the chamber, retrieves and then mates with Danae. Their coupling results in the birth of Perseus. Upon learning of this, Acrisius sends off Danae and Perseus to the open ocean in an ark, condemning them to certain death at the mercy of the waves. However, their ark eventually reaches the island of Serifos and they are adopted by a couple, the man being the brother of Polydectes, the king of Serifos.

When Perseus reached adulthood, he became a strong and handsome man. By this time, Polydectes wants Danae as a wife. Knowing that Perseus would come between him and Danae, Polydectes sends off Perseus to retrieve the head of Medusa, a task that the king knows is impossible.

Medusa, the only mortal out of once beautiful Gorgon sisters who were condemned by Athena to their monstrous appearance. Whilst Medusa retained her beautiful face, there is a heavy price to pay for whoever dares to gaze directly into her visage-- they would be turned to stone. Knowing that the task at hand was an impossible one, Perseus asks Hermes and Athena for assistance.

Together with a number of nymphs, Hermes and Athena provides Perseus a pair of winged sandals to fly him to the end of the world, where Medusa and the Gorgons lived. They also equip him with a mirrored shield and a sword. The mirrored shield would allow Perseus to look at Medusa without having to stare at her directly and suffer a terrible fate.

With the mirrored shield, Perseus is able to get near Medusa and kill her by decapitation. However, when he cuts off her head, her blood gives rise to two offspring: Chrysaor, a giant, winged boar, and Pegasus, a winged horse. Pegasus allows Perseus to flee the land of the Gorgons upon his back, and fly back home safely.

Perseus saves Andromeda:

On the way home from killing Medusa, Perseus encounters Andromeda, a beautiful woman, who is chained to some rocks. Andromeda tells him that her mother, Cassiopeia, had angered Poseidon by telling him that she was more beautiful than the Nereids who were part of Poseidon's court. Poseidon punished her mother by flooding the country, and sending a sea serpent to harass her people.

An oracle had advised King Cephus, who is Andromeda's father, that if he sacrificed her to a serpent, Poseidon would be appeased. Andromeda begs Perseus to save her and he agrees, but only on the condition that King Cephus gives him Andromeda's hand in marriage as reward for the deed. When the time came for the serpent to kill Andromeda, Perseus pounces on top of it, managing to slay the beast after a fierce battle. Perseus then frees Andromeda and returns to the palace with his new bride.

Perseus then learns that King Cephus had deceived him because had already promised to marry off Andromeda to Phineus. Phineus arrives with a small army to disrupt Perseus' and Andromeda's wedding. At this point, Perseus makes use of Medusa's head which he has kept in a bag; he pulls it out and turns it towards the advancing party, effectively turning Phineus and his army into stone.

When he gets home, Perseus finds out his mother is holed up in a religious site and in hiding from King Polydectes who still desires her. He warns King Polydectes that he still has Medusa's head in a bag and that he could use it against him. King Polydectes doubts this so Perseus pulls out Medusa's head, turning the King and all of his guests into stone.

The Story of Oedipus:

The story of Oedipus mostly came from writings by Sophocles. It was an often-retold story about human relations in all levels without the excessive violence that is the hallmark of most Greek mythology stories.

Oedipus was a king who ruled over Thebes, in what is now Boeotia, a city in central Greece. He was the son of Queen Jocasta and King Laius who consulted the Oracle at Delphi to determine if he would ever have children with the Queen. He was told that any son born from their union would end up murdering them both. Eventually, Queen Jocasta and King Laius managed to have a son. To avoid the prophecy, he orders his servants to pierce the baby's ankles to prevent him from crawling. They named the boy Oedipus, meaning "swollen foot".

To make doubly sure that Oedipus would not fulfil the prophecy, Queen Jocasta gives Oedipus to one of her shepherds and orders the servant to leave the baby in the mountains to die. The shepherd, however, felt sorry for the baby and so he hands the child over to the court of King

Polybus of Corinth and his queen, Merope who were childless. The royal couple decides to adopt Oedipus and raise him as their own child.

When Oedipus became an adult, he is told that King Polybus and Queen Merope were not his real parents. He goes to the Oracle at Delphi who tells him that he would eventually marry his mother after killing his father. Thinking that this meant he was prophesied to kill King Polybus and Queen Merope, he decides to go to Thebes instead of Corinth, fearing that he would fulfill prophecy. On the way to Thebes he encounters his biological father, King Laius who was about to see the Oracle at Delphi as well. Oedipus ends up in an argument with King Laius' charioteer and ends up killing both of them, hence fulfilling the Oracle's prophecy.

He then meets a monster Sphinx, who has been plaguing Thebes by destroying crops and killing any traveler who failed to answer their questions. The Sphinx asks Oedipus to answer the same riddle that it has asked other travelers before: *"What walks on four legs in the morning, two legs in the afternoon, and three legs in the evening?"* After thinking about the question carefully Oedipus gives the correct answer: **Man**. Man crawls on four legs as a baby, walks around on two legs as an adult, and uses a walking stick (a third leg) as an old man. The Sphinx, upset that the riddle was correctly answered throws itself off the rock it was sitting on and dies.

When Oedipus returns to Thebes, he is told by Creon, the acting king at Thebes that anyone who would be able to kill the Sphinx would marry the queen, Jocasta and become king. Not knowing that Jocasta is his mother, Oedipus marries her and together, they end up having four children: Antigone, Eteocles, Ismene, and Polynices.

Several years later as pestilence descends on Thebes, Oedipus sends Creon to the Oracle at Delphi to consult about what to do about the pestilence. The oracle tells him that the disasters are happening because Laius' killer has not been identified and caught. Oedipus then asks the prophet Tiresias to tell him who the killer was. Tiresias tells Oedipus that it was Oedipus himself that killed Laius, not realizing who the man was. After a heated argument between Creon and Oedipus, Jocasta tells them of their baby son and how he supposedly died when she ordered the shepherd to leave him to die in the mountains.

As they are arguing about the death of Laius, a messenger from Corinth arrives and tells everyone that King Polybus of Corinth has died. Upon hearing the news, Oedipus is relieved, still believing that Polybus is his real father and that the first prophecy he was given did not come true. He refuses to attend the funeral, however, in order to avoid meeting his adoptive mother as the second part of the prophecy may still come true.

The messenger however, also reveals to Oedipus that King Polybus and Queen Merope were only his adoptive parents. Learning this, Oedipus is crestfallen knowing that he had indeed killed his real father and married and impregnated his mother. He tries to see Queen Jocasta who has hanged herself. His grief pushed him to the edge of insanity, and taking a brooch from Jocasta's gown, he proceeds to blind himself. Eventually, Oedipus flees the city with his daughter Antigone as his guide, and reaches Athens where he meets and is welcomed by King Theseus. He dies in Athens a short time later.

Aesop's Fables

These are stories involving inanimate objects and animals that speak and are meant to convey moral lessons about life in general. Many of the stories have been used throughout the centuries as cautionary tales for questionable human behavior including, "The Boy Who Cried Wolf," and "The Tortoise and the Hare".

A story worth telling comes from the Iliad and involves the rift between a god and a mortal. Dionysus was travelling across Greece to make his cult known. In Thrace, King Lycurgus does not take too kindly of Dionysius' proselytizing and he imprisons the Maenads, followers of Dionysus. Dionysus flees before he can be taken prisoner and proceeds to exact revenge against Lycurgus. In Thetis, he sends a drought to Thrace which incites its people to rebellion against Lycurgus.

Dionysius, the god of madness, drives Lycurgus insane to the point that he mistakes his son to be a patch of ivy and slices him up. After an oracle claims that the drought in Thrace would continue if Lycurgus lived, his own people have him drawn and quartered. Following the death of Lycurgus, Dionysius lifts the drought curse.

Chapter 9.

Influences of Greek Mythology in Today's Culture

Greek mythology has pervaded almost every aspect of our daily lives in the modern age. We sometimes hear terms in science and technology, see brand names, watch television shows and movies, read all kinds of periodicals, use our gadgets, and not even realize that we are experiencing throwbacks to ancient Greek mythology.

Greek Mythology in Education and Learning

The study of Ancient Greece is a must for students and scholars of history, philosophy, archaeology, and literature. As the seat of human intellectual learning, the study of Ancient Greece is required because so much of their intellectual output continues to elicit discussion today. And because Greek scholarly work on the arts and sciences frequently allude to Greek mythology, understanding Greek mythology is essential in appreciating the thought process of the ancient Greeks.

Most universities, such as Harvard, offers courses with in-depth coverage of Greek mythology. Other major universities also have extensive offerings on teaching it. For example:

- *Ohio State University's Archaeology Department sponsors*

- extensive excavations of ancient Greek sites, and Greek mythology is an integral part of the theoretical classroom instruction that helps provide students with an understanding of Greek architecture and literature.
- Oxford University in England offers a 100-hour, 10-week credit course titled, "Greek Mythology". The course will give an exposition on their sources, how they should be interpreted, the source of their continuing influence, and its impact on history and learning.
- Cornell University in New York offers a course, "Greek Mythology" that puts the emphasis on the significance of mythology on Mediterranean society, the application of Greek mythology in the understanding of political and moral concepts, religion, and Greek literature, and the influences and factors involved in myth creation.

If mere immersion in Greek mythology is not sufficient for the interested student, the following schools offer degrees that feature a concentration on the subject:

- Seton Hall University: B.A., Major in Classical Studies
- University College Dublin: BA Evening Degree 2011/12 Greek and Roman Civilization
- University of Liverpool: Classical Studies BA (Hons)
- University of Texas San Antonio: Bachelor of Arts Degree in Classical Studies and   Humanities

Greek Mythology in Art and Exhibitions

The value of Greek mythology in acculturating the masses is

also considered an important part of general learning and knowledge. All the world's major museums have sections specifically appropriated for the relics of Greek mythology, but even smaller ones contain impressive exhibitions. The following are examples of these collections:

- The J. Paul Getty Museum in Los Angeles has had an ongoing exhibition since 206 showing copies of sculptures of deities such as Achilles, Aphrodite, Apollo, and Athena, and Hermes. The museum has also sponsored extensive conservation works on certain pieces of Greek mythology art. It also has a program package designed for K-12 instruction on Greek mythology.
- The American Museum of Natural History in New York City, New York houses permanent exhibits and interactive shows highlighting certain Greek mythology characters. They also have education programs for youngsters that focus on Greek mythology.
- The British Museum in London in the United Kingdom has many permanent exhibits of pieces portraying Greek mythology characters. They also have a permanent 45-minute presentation for youth, "School Spotlight Talk Presentation: Greek Myths".
- Of course, the most impressive and extensive collections are the ones in closest proximity to where Greek mythology originated: Greece.

Science and Technology

Many heavenly bodies are actually named after different

characters in Greek mythology. The planet Uranus is directly named after one of the original gods. Planets in our Solar System, such as Jupiter and Mars, whilst named after Roman gods, also have Greek counterpart names. Other instances where Greek mythology is invoked include:

- There are asteroids named after Greek gods: Persephone, Demeter, and Hephaestus;
- There are at least four elements in the periodic table named after Greek gods: Tantalum named after King Tantalus, Nobium named after his daughter Niobe, Promethium named after Prometheus, and titanium named after the Titans;
- The United States program named the space program that included the first moon landing after the god Apollo;
- The Trojan Horse in modern language also refers to a computer code that on the surface appears harmless but contains a harmful computer virus that is unleashed when a certain condition or command is entered;
- The mother of Greek gods, Gaia has an important chemical process named after her: The Gaia hypothesis theorizes that live organisms interact with their inorganic elements in a complex, a self-regulating mechanism that helps maintain conditions for life on the Earth.

Greek Mythology in Entertainment and Media

With the head-spinning advances in technology over the past few years, a lot of focus has been placed on how people receive information and entertainment. Just a generation ago, entertainment meant going to the local cinema to watch a movie or sitting in front of a television. This is not the case these days. Those in the entertainment business are aware that people can watch what they want whenever they want on tablets and phones. The more interesting or attention-grabbing something is, the better are its prospects for profit and popularity.

Greek mythology is a subject matter often used in many popular entertainment mediums. From books to movies, it is a theme that is used and re-used quite often. There is a lot of action, drama, interesting characters, horrifying entities, beautiful women, and heroic figures in Greek mythology. There is also no shortage of story lines for its many heroes and villains.

There have been countless representations of Greek mythology in popular media just over the past fifty years. These have taken the form of books, movies, plays, and television shows that have garnered mass appeal and audiences worldwide in several languages. In this chapter I will provide a small but representative sample of entertainment media and products based on Greek mythology.

Movies and television

The following is a partial list of major movie productions that were based on the characters, stories and traditions of Greek mythology. For every movie listed here, there are at least the same number of movies that have Greek mythology themes or have appropriated certain characters and events. The favorite character seems to be that of Herakles or Hercules which has spawned the following movies:

1. Hercules (1958) starring Steve Reeves
2. Hercules Unchained (1959) starring Steve Reeves
3. Hercules Vs the Hydra (1960) co-starring Jayne Mansfield
4. Hercules and the Captive Women (1961)
5. The Fury of Hercules, (1962)
6. Hercules Vs. The Giant Warrior, (1964)
7. Hercules, the Avenger, (1965)
8. Hercules and the Amazon Women, (1994) TV movie
9. Hercules and the Circle of Fire 1994 TV movie
10. Hercules and the Lost Kingdom 1994 TV movie
11. Hercules in the Underworld 1994 TV movie
12. Hercules in the Maze of the Minotaur 1994 TV movie
13. Hercules: The Legendary Journeys (1995-1999) TV series
14. Hercules (1997) animated Walt Disney movie
15. The Amazing Feats of Young Hercules (1997) animated
16. Young Hercules (1998)
17. Young Hercules (1998–99) United States - TV series
18. Hercules and Xena - 1999 animated
19. Hercules 2005 TV miniseries
20. The Legend of Hercules United States
21. Hercules (2014) United States
22. Other movies depicting other characters of Greek mythology:
23. The Odyssey (1997)
24. The Animated Odyssey 2000 animated TV movie
25. Helen of Troy (2003)
26. Troy (2004)

GREEK MYTHOLOGY | 65

27. Jason and the Argonauts (1963)
28. Jason and the Argonauts (2000) TV mini-series
29. The Spirit (2008) United States - features the Golden Fleece and the blood of Heracles.
30. Oedipus Rex (1957)
31. Oedipus Rex (1967)
32. Oedipus the King (1968)
33. Clash of the Titans (1981)
34. Clash of the Titans (2010)
35. Wrath of the Titans (2012)

There are also many movies and television series that have featured the Amazons.

1. The Amazons (1917), an American silent movie
2. Amazons (1984)
3. Amazons (1986), an Argentine adventure fantasy
4. Wonder Woman (1975-1979), a television series
5. Wonder Woman (2009) an animated film
6. Wonder Woman (2011 TV pilot), a 2011 television pilot
7. Wonder Woman (2017)

There is also a great number of comics and electronic games based on Greek characters and events.

Notable product branding and signage

The following products and product lines are based on Greek mythology:

- Aetna – A major insurance company named after the daughter of Uranus and Gaia;
- Ajax detergent – Named after Ajax, who was a Greek

warrior famous for his participation in the Trojan War;
- Amazon.com – Online ordering service, named after the female warrior amazons;
- Canon EOS SLR camera – Named after Eos, the goddess of dawn.
- Cerberus Capital Management, L.P. – The largest private equity company in the world is named after one of the guards of the Underworld;
- Hermes – Luxury apparel line named after the messenger god.
- Nike – Named after Nike, the Greek goddess of victory;
- Olympus Cameras – Japanese company named after the residence of the gods;
- Oracle – One of the world's largest software companies;
- Orion – Major movie production company and named after a great huntsman.
- Pandora – Beauty and make-up conglomerate;
- Readers Digest, the movie studio TriStar Pictures, B.F. Goodyear tires, and Mobil Oil have used the Pegasus, the winged horse as their corporate logo;

Psychology

Perhaps the most famous Greek mythology character in the field of psychoanalysis is Oedipus where the condition Oedipus Complex comes from. Originally coined by Sigmund Freud, the condition refers to ideas and emotions rooted in the subconscious that is manifested by a child's desire to sexually possess his or her mother, and killing their father. There is also a "Medea Complex" used to denote a condition where parents desire to harm or even murder their offspring.

Conclusion

When we immerse ourselves in Greek mythology, we sometimes lose sight of the fact that everything we are reading about is purely fiction. While there have been recent discoveries possibly suggesting that much of the Trojan War was actual historical fact, the gods and goddesses described in Greek mythology are, at their essence, simple figments of the of the imagination of the Ancient Greeks. But even as imaginary narratives they have brought so much color and excitement to human civilization over the past 2,000 years or so.

Greek mythology is not just a collection of myths. They are stories that show us how our ancestors lived and thought in their day, their morality, and their priorities. The myths and fables are also windows to the human psyche: emotions, thoughts, and feelings that we all have.

The "myths" provide us with an invaluable glimpse of who we are as human beings. We have seen that the gods that the ancient Greeks invented had as much if not more moral and character flaws and weaknesses than the humans had dominion over. After all, if gods could have human shortcomings, what should be expected of mere mortals?

We are outraged when Zeus treats mortals like throwaway rags, and feel the triumph of Perseus as he severs Medusa's head. We revel at humankind's hubris, and folly of the major characters. We find amusement in the fact that even the gods have flaws and weaknesses which may sometimes become their undoing as well. A lot can be learned from these myths including lessons and warnings that we can apply to our daily lives. They are fiction, but fiction that is still useful in the modern age.

Ultimately, however, who can say that these fictional belief systems of the ancient Greeks are unfounded factually and spiritually? Christians, Jews, Hindus and Muslims have their own belief systems that focus on inanimate deities that they allow to affect their lives. If we transported a time traveler from ancient Athens to today's world, he or she may look at organized religion in its current state and consider them just as unbelievable as their Zeus, Poseidon, Apollo, etc.

While we can debate the historical, moral, and spiritual values of Greek mythology, there is one non-debatable aspect: That Greek mythology has made significant contributions to our lives as it has added so much depth and texture to mankind's inventory of classic and modern literature and culture. It has permeated human lives in the form of compelling stories and symbols all the way to today's entertainment and escapism. While we may not believe that Zeus, Ares, Aphrodite and the Titans really existed, we can surely stay in the moment and enjoy them in our imaginations.

www.ingramcontent.com/pod-product-compliance
Lightning Source LLC
Chambersburg PA
CBHW071032080526
44587CB00015B/2589